Rolling Right Along

By Sue Bursztynski

Harcourt Achieve

Rigby • Saxon • Steck-Vaughn

www.HarcourtAchieve.com
1.800.531.5015

PM Extensions Nonfiction

Sapphire

U.S. Edition © 2013 HMH Supplemental Publishers
10801 N. MoPac Expressway
Building #3
Austin, TX 78759
www.hmhsupplemental.com

Text © 2005 Cengage Learning Australia Pty Limited
Photographs and illustrations © 2005 Cengage Learning Australia Pty Limited
Originally published in Australia by Cengage Learning Australia

6 7 8 9 10   1957   16 15 14
4500462304

Text: Sue Bursztynski
Reprint: Siew Han Ong
Printed in China by 1010 Printing International Ltd

Acknowledgments

The author and publisher would like to acknowledge permission to reproduce material from the following sources: Photographs by AAP Image, p. 27 bottom; akg2, pp. 21, 22; APL/Corbis/Bettmann, p. 14/ Giedeon/Mendel, p. 18 centre; Index Stock Imagery, cover inset/ pp. 12, 23, 28 top right; Mary Evans Online, pp. 23 top, 27 top; Newspix, pp. 17 bottom, 30 left; photolibrary.com, cover, pp. 4 top, 4 centre, 4 bottom, 5 left, 13 top, 13 bottom, 19 top, 19 bottom, 29 left, 29 top right, 29 bottom right, 30 centre right; Photos.com, pp. 13 centre, 17 top, 28 bottom right; Photo Edit Inc., pp. 30 top right, 30 bottom centre; Picture-desk.com/Kobal Collection, p. 18 bottom; Science Photo Library, pp. 11 left, 11 right.

Rolling Right Along

ISBN 978 0 75 789261 5

Contents

Wheels
within Wheels

When you hear the word *wheel*, what do you think of? Cars, bikes, and other forms of transportation? The wheel has played a very important part in the history of transportation since it was invented in Mesopotamia about 5,500 years ago. It has made all the difference in being able to reach places quickly and has influenced what goods can be produced and sold. Train wheels made a huge difference in the 19th century.

Did you know?

The South and Central American civilizations found that the wheel just wasn't practical, and they managed well without it. The Egyptians had the wheel and stopped using it when they decided that pack-carrying animals suited them better for transportation.

THE SPINNING JENNY.

The wheel is used for much more than transportation. It has been a vital part of our lives for thousands of years. Improvements in the wheel helped people find new ways of doing things.

For example more pottery was needed at one time for bigger populations. The invention of the pottery wheel was the solution. For centuries, women spun thread for cloth on sticks called *spindles*. When more thread was needed, the spinning wheel came along. This must have been a very important achievement: think of all the fairy tales in which a spinning wheel plays a part! An improvement in that wheel, the spinning jenny, completely changed the lifestyles of many country people, who had to go to town and work in factories.

Let's take a short tour through the history of this simple but important invention. Rolling on . . .

Origins
of the Wheel

Imagine a world with no wheels. There are no roads, and therefore no cars or even carts. No one turns pottery on a wheel or spins thread on a spinning wheel. Then one day, someone has a bright idea and the world is changed forever.

Letter to the King of Uruk

To Gilgamesh, Lord of Uruk

Greetings!

As Your Majesty ordered, I have examined the new device, brought to the city market this morning. A farmer uses a box that rolls to carry his goods for sale.

He calls it a "cart," and the round wooden disks which move it, "wheels." As he explained to me, he split a log, made planks, and cut three slices for each "wheel." These are hammered together and attached to rods called "axles." Pegs hold the wheels in place underneath the box. The wheels and axles turn and move the cart, which is pulled by an ox. The farmer said the ox was already pulling his plow, so why not his cart?

It is indeed impressive, Sire. The merchants to whom I spoke had no interest in the idea since they have pack animals. But I believe we can make use of this idea, perhaps using swift donkeys rather than oxen. We would need to build artificial tracks on which to run them if we are to use them properly. However, if we can find a way to make the cart and wheel lighter, it would be highly effective. A warrior could shoot arrows or throw spears while a comrade drove the donkeys. A cart like this would also increase the speed with which our armies could travel, giving us a huge advantage over our enemies.

This afternoon I will bring the farmer and his cart to the palace to show you, but will send this tablet ahead with a swift messenger.

Your Majesty's loyal servant,

General Enkidu

Mesopotamian wheels

The wheel is thought to have been invented in Mesopotamia, in what is now Iraq, about 5,500 years ago. Unfortunately wood doesn't last that long, so we don't have any original wheels left, but there are ancient pictures of Sumerian **chariots** with heavy-looking wooden wheels. There were solid disk wheels in Northern countries, but the Mesopotamian ones were made up of three pieces. Later the heavy wooden wheels were replaced by lighter metal ones with spokes.

As with a lot of modern technology, war was the reason for improving the wheel. Better wheels meant that chariots could be lighter and could travel more quickly. Metal (bronze) tires around the rims kept them from wearing out. But metalworking technology had to be improved first.

Imagine what it must have been like to be an enemy of the first Sumerian king who had these travel devices and to see them rushing toward you on the battlefield!

Bicycles

When German Baron von Drais began riding a wheeled machine around his gardens for exercise in 1817, he wasn't the first—a Frenchman had built one in 1790. But the baron's bicycle was unique: it was steerable.

The "hobbyhorse" or "Draisienne" was nothing like your modern mountain bike with its multiple speeds and gears. It was wooden and had no pedals. It was more like a scooter you could ride. Still it was very popular in the early 1800s.

Bicycles continued to develop as people experimented. In 1860, a French hobbyhorse repairman, Pierre Michaud, was fixing a bicycle when he got the bright idea of attaching pedals to it. It still wasn't much like the bicycles we know today, but riders didn't have to push any more. It was nicknamed "boneshaker" because the awful roads of the time made it very uncomfortable to ride.

Tires became metal, then solid rubber. In 1888, a Scottish veterinarian, John Boyd Dunlop, made some air-filled tires for his young son's tricycle. His experiment made a huge difference in the way wheels could now be used.

John Dunlop

Dunlop and a bicycle with air-filled tires

The most famous nineteenth century bike was the "penny-farthing," which had a large and a small wheel. Although popular with young men, the bike had its drawbacks. It was hard to mount, very unsteady and unsuitable for women in long dresses. Also, it was costly because it had to be custom-made to fit the rider's leg length. In fact, this bike cost the average person six months' pay! Obviously, less expensive bikes had to be developed before many could ride.

So next time you go on your paper route or ride to school, remember how far the bicycle has come in nearly two centuries!

Did you know?

*There are over 8 million bicycles in Beijing, the capital of China. In Denmark bikes are used for 20–30 percent of daily city travel. In Asia, bicycle-powered **rickshaws** are used for 10–20 percent of carrying goods. Early motorbikes had pedals that worked in the same way as a bicycle.*

Ferris Wheel

"The wild man with wheels in his head": George Ferris and his invention

New Attraction at World's Fair

By Samuel Smith

Chicago, June 16, 1893

Engineer George Ferris has built the main attraction of the World's Fair which opens in a few days, a fairground ride to be named after him—the "Ferris whee

"It all began a couple of years ago when we attended an engineers' banquet," explained Mr. Ferris's wife, Margaret, who was beautifully dressed in black and gold for the occasion. "They were already planning an event to celebrate the four-hundredth anniversary of Columbus's landing in America. After all, if the French could have their Paris Exhibition to celebrate the centenary of their Revolution, why couldn't we celebrate *our* big event? Someone complained that while the French had the **Eiffel Tower** at their Exhibition, we had nothing to outdo it. 'And what's so special about the Eiffel Tower, anyway?' my husband argued. 'It's just a bridge turned sideways. We can do better than that, surely.' "

Mr. Ferris had been doodling on a table napkin, drawing a merry-go-round carousel, which he turned on its side. Then he took his napkin up to the main table and showed it to the men there, suggesting that they could use cars instead of horses. They became very excited by the idea.

However, it nearly didn't happen. Mrs. Ferris said, "At first the organizers of the fair agreed to give George the concession in the fair grounds. Then they realized exactly what he had in mind and nearly cancelled the plan. They said he was some sort of a wild man with wheels in his head! But finally he plan was organized, and they started building."

The wheel is an impressive 250 feet in **diameter** and has a **circumference** of 825 feet, with a 45-foot-long axle, the largest single piece of forged metal in the world. There are thirty-six cars, each of which can hold six people. Two engines, each of a thousand **horsepower**, turn the gigantic wheel. Each car goes slowly up until the entire city can be seen from a height of 266 feet in the air.

The view from the top is spectacular. It made all forty members of the invited party gasp with pleasure. Mrs. Ferris opened a bottled drink, climbed up on a chair, and toasted her husband and the success of his wheel.

On Thursday, the wheel opens to the public at fifty cents a ride. It will be there for the whole of the fair.

Did you know?

There are two modern giant Ferris wheels: one at the Prater Amusement Park in Austria and one in London, England, which is the Millenium Wheel. The Prater Park has had a wheel since 1897, not long after the original one was built in Chicago. It is 200 feet high and can carry hundreds of people. Its cars are big enough to host large functions. The London wheel, also known as "The London Eye," was built in 1999 and has become a major tourist attraction.

Pottery Wheels

Before the wheel, potters used to rest the base of a pot on a flat bowl, which they turned. Although this method is still used in some countries, it is slow. Once villages grew into towns and trade expanded, more pottery was needed. There had to be a faster way of turning pots around as they were sculpted.

Clay

Floor

Flat bowl that manually spur by potter

The first actual pictures of pottery wheels are seen in Egyptian wall paintings from over 4,400 years ago. The wheels were pictured on stands, which made them easier to turn. Like pottery wheels everywhere, the early wheels were made of wood. With one hand, a potter turned the wheel to spin long coils of clay. With the other hand, the potter shaped and smoothed the clay into pots.

Much later, the ancient Greeks came up with a design known as the *kick-wheel* in which the foot could be used to turn the pottery wheel from below. At last, both of the potters' hands were free to shape the pots. By the sixteenth century, potters in Europe were using a high **turntable** with a large wheel underneath for the feet to move. This method continued until the nineteenth century.

Most modern wheels are electric. Potters use the method known as "throwing," which involves placing clay in the middle and working on their creation while the wheel spins. However some modern potters enjoy using the earlier method of spinning the wheel by hand or foot. Pots can be thrown on these wheels as long as the wheel is spinning. The wheel has to be kicked again as soon as it begins to spin slower.

It is amazing how much people have been able to do with a little imagination and a simple disk!

Did you know?

Potters were highly respected in ancient Egypt, where there was even a Festival of the Potter's Wheel. It was believed that the ram-headed Khnum created humans on his pottery wheel.

Spinning Wheels

Mr. James Hargreaves Speaks: an interview with our correspondent in London, England, 1768.

I spoke to James Hargreaves—inventor of a new machine called the *spinning jenny* at his home in Blackburn, England. Mr. Hargreaves won the weaving industry's competition to create a faster means of spinning thread. It will be used in the exciting new cloth factories.

Q. Mr. Hargreaves, thank you for your time, and congratulations. You must be proud to now be building the machine you designed some fourteen years ago.

A. Thank you, sir, but I'm not sure it's such a good thing. The local spinners have been standing in front of my home in protest. My family and I have had to move to Nottingham, England.

Q. Dear me, aren't people over-reacting?

A. To me, they are. I understand the anger of the people who have been spinning at home. This machine only needs one person to run it and does the work eight people did before. These people will now be out of work. Some will get jobs in the factories, others will not. But they must understand that the weaving industry needs more thread. They just can't produce it quickly enough at home.

Q. Could you describe the spinning jenny for our readers?

A. It's a treadle-powered spinning wheel that can operate several spindles. One person can make them all turn at once, producing more thread than on a normal wheel.

Q. Would you like to take us through a history of spinning until the present day and suggest some possible improvements in the future?

A. Certainly. Most spinning until the early **Middle Ages** was done with spindles and distaffs. These were two sticks. The distaff, held wool which was spun onto the spindle. The weight on the bottom of the spindle is called the *whorl*. It makes spinning easier. A skilled spindle spinner can do as well as one using a wheel.

Here in England, we had the great wheel, called a *walking-wheel*. We first started using it in the fourteenth century, though it was being used in France and other parts of Europe in the thirteenth century. It was turned with one hand and the thread drawn out with the other. The worker had to step forward to draw out the thread each time—not very comfortable! Some English spinners "walked" about thirty miles a week.

The Saxony wheel is turned by a treadle so that the spinner can sit and work with freed hands. It was invented in the fifteenth century and I understand it is very popular in the American colonies.

The future? I don't know. Perhaps a spinning jenny that controls more spindles? I hear somebody is already designing one called the *spinning mule*.

Q. Good luck, Mr. Hargreaves!

Did you know?

The Indian flag has a spinning wheel on it! is is the charkha, which is still used in ny parts of Asia. It has spokes but no rim, ly ropes around the edges. The spinner sits the ground and turns the handle, spinning e thread on to a spindle. The flag's design s the idea of independence leader Gandhi ctured below), who had his own charkha.

Chapter 6

The *Wheel* in the Modern World

Take a walk down the street. Look around you. Wheeled cars, bikes, and scooters whiz past. Your wind-up watch has wheels in it. When you put on your in-line skates or step on to your skateboard, think of the wheels that are helping you enjoy yourself. Your CDs and tapes spin while they play—like wheels. Inside the players are even more wheels. At the supermarket, wheeled carts make carrying groceries easier.

The **turbines** that power **hydroelectric plants**, planes, and ships are wheels. They came from the water-wheels that used the pushing power of streams or waterfalls to help grind flour. There were wheels in the first televisions and calculators. Gears—little toothed wheels—are still a vital part of machinery.

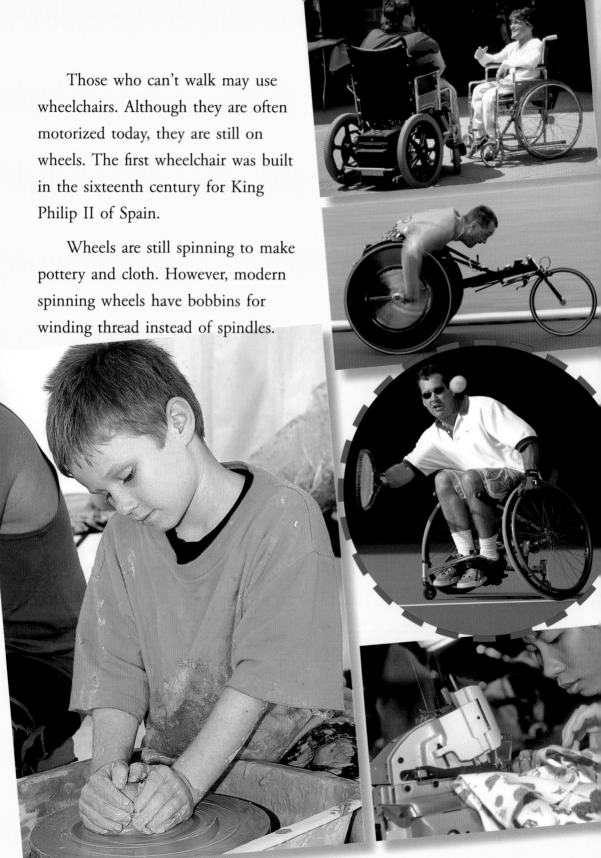

Those who can't walk may use wheelchairs. Although they are often motorized today, they are still on wheels. The first wheelchair was built in the sixteenth century for King Philip II of Spain.

Wheels are still spinning to make pottery and cloth. However, modern spinning wheels have bobbins for winding thread instead of spindles.

Did you know?

In the Middle Ages, the wheel was a symbol of how life could change for people. There were many paintings of the Wheel of Fortune, showing people reaching the top (success), while others plunged to the bottom (despair). Everyone, it was believed, was tied to this "lucky" wheel and would reach the top or bottom sooner or later.

We speak of "the wheels of industry" or "the wheels of justice." Someone who works hard is putting their "shoulder to the wheel" or "nose to the grindstone" (a wheel that sharpens tools).

The wheel is still with us and will be for a long time to come.

Glossary

chariot A two-wheeled transport that was used in ancient times for battle and for racing. It was pulled by horses or, in Mesopotamia, by donkeys.

circumference The distance around a circle

diameter The distance across a circle

Eiffel Tower A cast-iron tower in Paris, France that became a tourist attraction. It was built for the Paris World Fair of 1889.

horsepower A unit of power, used to describe how powerful an engine is. One horsepower is equal to 550 pounds (250 kg) being lifted (or pulled) one foot in a second

hydroelectric plant A place where electricity is generated using the pushing power of water

Middle Ages A period of time from around the year 1000 to the year 1500

rickshaw A small, two-wheeled carriage pulled by a person, either on foot or riding a bicycle

turbine A type of motor powered by gas or water. It is made up of wheels.

turntable A rotating disk or platform. Turntables can be used as a bench for making pottery, and can spin a CD or a record that plays music.